TeamWorks:
Spiritual Life of the Leaders

Craig Kennet Miller

DISCIPLESHIP MINISTRIES
The United Methodist Church

Spiritual Life of the Leaders **is part of the TeamWorks series**

For more information on how your church, district, and conference can be involved, visit

www.TeamWorksUMC.org

TeamWorks Developer:

Craig Kennet Miller is the Director of Congregational Development at Discipleship Ministries of the United Methodist Church. He is the author of numerous books including *iKids: Parenting in the Digital Age* and *Boomer Spirituality: Seven Values for the Second Half of Life*. He serves on the design team of the School of Congregational Development, is an Elder in the Cal-Pac Conference of the UMC, and has a Doctor of Ministry Degree from Fuller Theological Seminary.

For more information, please contact:
Craig Kennet Miller
Discipleship Ministries
cmiller@umcdiscipleship.org
615-340-7081

Discipleship Ministries of The United Methodist Church
P.O Box 340003
Nashville, TN
37203

Index

Schedule for the *TeamWorks: Spiritual Life of the Leader* seminars and MyWork devotions

Schedule Template

Use the template below to schedule your sessions. TeamWorks Seminars are designed for 2-hours. You also can do a one day format, with participants using the MyWork devotions to follow-up their experience. Plan for 4-hours with a break for a meal or refreshments.

Session	Date	Topic
Seminar One	_____	**Spiritual Life Template**
MyWork 1	_____	What Are My Spiritual Practices?
MyWork 2	_____	The Door
MyWork 3	_____	The Essentials
MyWork 4	_____	Discovering My Spiritual Gifts
Seminar Two	_____	**Our Giftedness Together**

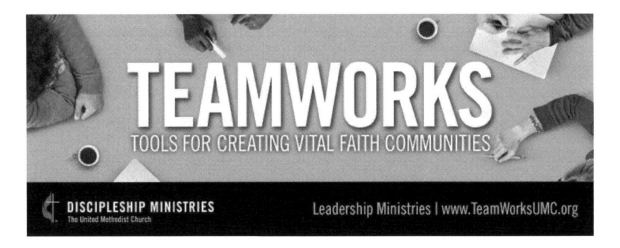

Welcome to TeamWorks

As a participant in *TeamWorks: Spiritual Life of the Leader*, you are taking a bold step in your faith for the future of your congregation. You are committing yourself to focus on your spiritual life and how you work with others.

How to Use this Study

This study contains material each team member needs to participate in the *The Spiritual Life of the Leader*. It contains the following material:

1. **Seminar Presentations:** Here you will find the presentation material for two TeamWorks Seminars that will be shared when you meet as a group. The material includes presentation slides, space for taking notes, and discussion questions.

2. **MyWork**: The MyWork material is designed for your personal study and reflection as a follow-up to the seminars.

3. **TeamWorks Tools**: At the end of this study guide, you will find a variety of articles and templates that you will use both as an individual and as a team.

TeamWorks Design

This study is designed to be offered as two separate 2-hour seminars with time in between for participants to do personal study and reflection using the MyWork devotions between the seminars. Use the *Schedule Template* on the previous page to plan your time.

You also can offer this as a one-day experience lasts 4-hours. You will need to provide a break for individual time for participants to do *MyWork 4: Spiritual Gifts.* Participants will do the MyWork devotions and reading as a follow-up to the one-day experience.

Full Participation

Participants are encouraged to commit to attending both seminars and to do MyWork devotions and read the "Spiritual Life of the Leaders" article between *Seminar One: Spiritual Life Template* and *Seminar Two: Our Giftedness Together*. If this is offered as a one-day experience, participants are encouraged read the material that was not covered on their own.

Instructions for Seminar Leaders:

TeamWorks Seminars are designed to encourage discussion. To prepare for each seminar do as follows:

1. Setup a room with table and chairs where groups of participants will interact during the seminars.
2. You will need an LCD projector and a screen or a large TV that can be hooked up to a computer to show the presentations.
3. Download the presentation slides from www.TeamWorksUMC.org. You may get them as a PDF or in PowerPoint. When using PowerPoint use it in presentation mode so you can view the notes for each slide.
4. Before leading a seminar, go to www.TeamWorksUMC.org and watch the Seminar Leaders Webinar for the seminar you are leading. The webinar will go through each slide and will offer tips and ideas for how to lead the seminar.
5. Set dates for the seminars or for the one-day experience.
6. Recruit a group of participants who will agree to attend both seminars and to do the MyWork devotions.

Set-up for the Seminars

Spiritual Life Seminar 1: Spiritual Life Template
Room: Room with tables and chairs for your participants
Equipment: Computer connected to an LCD Projector or screen
Materials: Copy of *TeamWorks: Spiritual Life of the Leaders* for each person
Downloads: Download presentation slides for *Spiritual Life Seminar 1* (PowerPoint or PDF)

Note: Participants will need to take the *Spiritual Gifts Assessment Tool* found in MyWorks 4 before participating in the next seminar (p. 30).

Futurecasting Seminar 2: Our Giftedness Together
Same room and equipment setup as above
Materials: Copy of *TeamWorks: Spiritual Life of the Leader* for each person
Downloads: Download presentation slides for *Spiritual Life 2* (PowerPoint or PDF)

TeamWorks Guidebooks and Tools

TeamWorks: Spiritual life of the Leader	• Encourage spiritual growth with the *Spiritual Life Template* • Maximize your teams giftedness by discovering spiritual gifts
TeamWorks: Connecting to Your Community	• Learn how new arrivals in your community seek *Homeland* • Use the *NICHE Process* to learn about your community
TeamWorks: Creating a Discipleship System	• Find out where your church fits on the *Lifecycle of the Church* • Use the *Settings for Ministry* to form a discipleship system
TeamWorks: Futurecasting	• Learn how to use the powerful *VAP-IT Strategic Planning Tool* • Use the *TeamWorks Church Assessment* to plan for the future

Discipleship Ministries   www.TeamWorksUMC.org

What's in a TeamWorks Guidebook?

Two 2-Hour Seminars	Four MyWorks Devotions
Two Tools for congregational life	Support at www.TeamWorksUMC.org

TeamWorks

Discipleship Ministries   www.TeamWorksUMC.org

SPIRITUAL LIFE OF THE LEADER
Seminar 1: Spiritual Life Template

B
O f Christ
D
Y

I Corinthians 12

Discipleship Ministries   www.TeamWorksUMC.org

Blessed to serve

Now there are varieties of gifts, but the same Spirit; and there are varieties of service, but the same Lord; and there are varieties of activities, but it is the same God who activates all or them in every one. To each is given the manifestation of the Spirit for the common good.

I Corinthians 12:4-7

Discipleship Ministries   www.TeamWorksUMC.org

ne in the spirit

For just as the body is one and has many members, and all the members of the body, though many, are one body, so it is with Christ. For in the one Spirit we were all baptized into one body—Jews or Greeks, slaves or free—and we were all made to drink of one Spirit. Indeed, the body does not consist of one member but of many.

I Corinthians 12:12-14

Discipleship Ministries   www.TeamWorksUMC.org

Designed to work together

But as it is, God arranged the members in the body, each one of them, as he chose. If all were a single member, where would the body be? As it is, there are many members, yet one body.

I Corinthians 12:18-20

Yielded for the common good

But God has so arranged the body, giving the greater honor to the inferior member, that there may be no dissension within the body, but the members may have the same care for one another. If one member suffers, all suffer together with it; if one member is honored, all rejoice together with it.

I Corinthians 12:24-26

Discussion 1

As a member of the Body of Christ, which of these instructions

- **inspires you most?**
- **is hardest for you to do?**

B_lessed_ **to serve**

O_ne_ **in the spirit**

D_esigned_ **to work together**

Y_ielded_ **for the common good**

Discipleship Ministries   www.TeamWorksUMC.org

But without ove ...

And now faith, hope, and love abide, these three; and the greatest of these is love.

I Corinthians 13:13

Discipleship Ministries   www.TeamWorksUMC.org

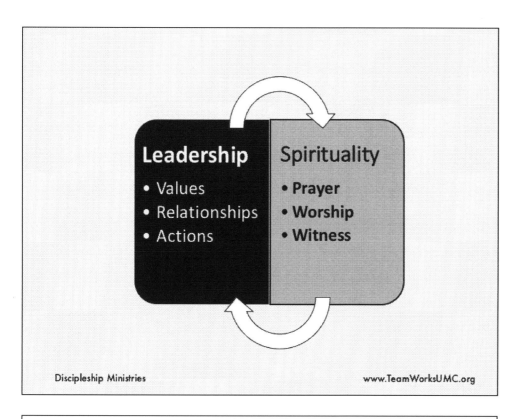

Discipleship Ministries   www.TeamWorksUMC.org

 Discussion 2

- What beliefs or spiritual practices are the most important to leaders in your congregation?
- What beliefs or spiritual practices are the most important to newcomers to your church?

Discipleship Ministries   www.TeamWorksUMC.org

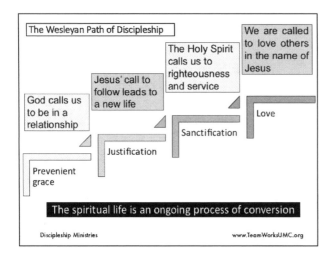

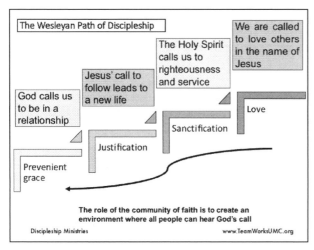

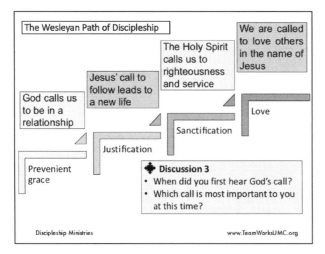

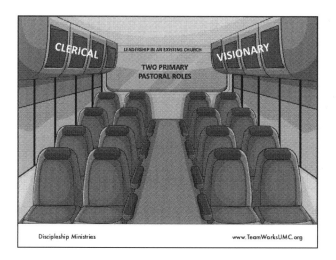

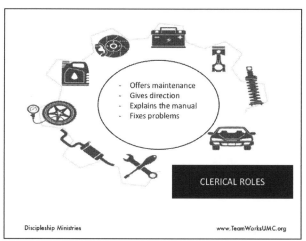

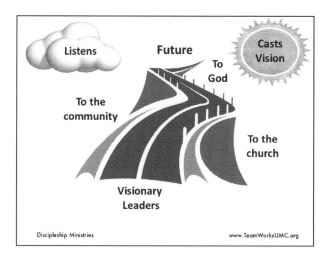

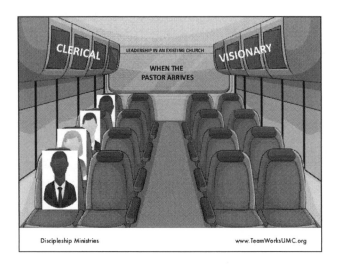

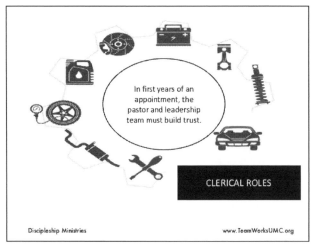

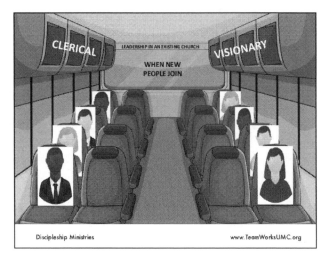

New people will see the pastor as visionary leader, while those who were there before the pastor will view the pastor as the cleric.

Discipleship Ministries   www.TeamWorksUMC.org

Discipleship Ministries — www.TeamWorksUMC.org

Get the Right People on the Bus

"We expected to find that the first step in taking a company from good to great would be to set a new direction, a new vision and strategy for the company...but the executives who ignited the transformation did not first figure out where to drive the bus and get people to take it there. No, they *first* got the right people on the bus (and the wrong people off it) and *then* figured out where to drive it."

 Jim Collins, *Good to Great*, p. 41

Discipleship Ministries — www.TeamWorksUMC.org

Discussion 4

- What has been the appointment history of pastors in your church?

- What is important about the clerical roles?

- Why does a church need visionary leadership?

- How are you creating a healthy leadership cohort? (getting the right people on the bus)

Discipleship Ministries — www.TeamWorksUMC.org

The spiritual life of leaders influence all aspects of congregational life

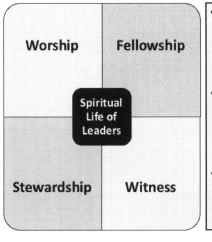

- The key to growth and vitality is a strong cohort of leaders whose spiritual life is a witness to others.

- Strong spiritual leaders attract newcomers who want to learn how to live the Christian life.

- Vital congregations establish normative expectations for the spiritual practices of their leaders.

Discipleship Ministries   www.TeamWorksUMC.org

The spiritual life of leaders influence all aspects of congregational life

- United Methodists view the spiritual life as an ongoing process.

- The early Methodists believed spiritual disciplines, such as Wesley's Means of Grace, formed the life of a Christian.

- Spiritual growth is fostered by being accountable to others for your spiritual life.

Discipleship Ministries   www.TeamWorksUMC.org

Intro to the Spiritual Life Template

The Spiritual Life Template is a tool for sharing your spiritual journey with a group. This can be used in a small group, leadership team, Bible study, accountability group, committee, or other such group that meets on an ongoing basis.

Three basic principles:
1. The spiritual life is one that is shared
2. Each individual decides for themselves what they want to share
3. The tool is used every time the group meets

Discipleship Ministries   www.TeamWorksUMC.org

Question 1: In which spiritual discipline(s) do you want to grow?

• One of the foundational aspects of United Methodist Christians is the way they approach the spiritual life as an ongoing process of growth and maturity.

• The early Methodists talked about Wesley's Means of Grace, that through the practice of spiritual disciplines a believer's life is formed in Christ.

• In the earliest forms, Methodists met on a regular basis in classes to hold one another accountable for the way they were growing in faith and practice.

Discipleship Ministries   www.TeamWorksUMC.org

Spiritual Life Questions

1. In which spiritual discipline(s) do you want to grow?

___ **Weekly worship**
___ **Daily Bible reading**
___ **Daily prayer**
___ **Frequency of communion:**
___ **Weekly** ___ **Monthly** ___ **Other**
___ **Service to others**
___ **Fasting or abstinence**
___ **Tithing/Giving**
___ **Family prayer**
Other:

Tip: How does your church teach & mentor people in these disciplines?

Wesley's Means of Grace

- The public worship of God
- The ministry of the Word, either read or expounded
- The Lord's Supper
- Family and private prayer
- Searching the Scriptures
- Fasting or abstinence
- Christian conferencing

Discipleship Ministries   www.TeamWorksUMC.org

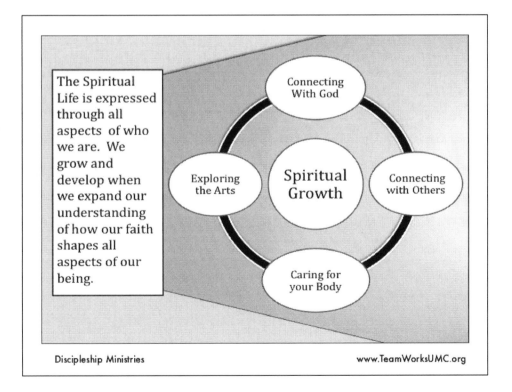

The Spiritual Life is expressed through all aspects of who we are. We grow and develop when we expand our understanding of how our faith shapes all aspects of our being.

Discipleship Ministries   www.TeamWorksUMC.org

Question 2: What is your plan for continued spiritual growth and development?

- **How do you connect with God?**
  Christianity is about having a relationship with God through our faith in Jesus Christ. Our relationship with God is key to our personal vitality.

- **How are you connecting with others?**
  Each moment we spend with another person is an opportunity to share in the grace of the moment. We need others to shape us and to form us into mature followers of Jesus Christ.

- **What arts feed your soul?**
  The Creator has equipped us to be creative. Take time to develop your artistic side – it will both feed you and connect you to others.

- **How are you taking care of your body?**
  The way we take care of our bodies affects every aspect of our relationship to God and to others. Exercise and healthy eating enhances our ability to be effective in ministry.

Discipleship Ministries   www.TeamWorksUMC.org

Spiritual Life Questions

2. What is your plan for your continued spiritual growth and development?

How do you connect with God?	How are you connecting with others?
___ Day apart ___ Worship ___ Meeting with a prayer partner or coach ___ Family prayer ___ Daily devotion ___ Other: _____	___ Time alone with spouse or friend ___ Focused time with your children ___ Regular connection with extended family ___ Prayer or accountability group ___ Time with friends outside of church ___ Other: _____
What arts feed your soul?	**How are you taking care of your body?**
___ Playing a musical instrument or singing ___ Writing ___ Drawing ___ Cooking ___ Dance ___ Gardening ___ Acting ___ Other: _____	___ Walking/running ___ Active in a sport ___ Healthy diet ___ Yoga/Pilates ___ Other: _____

Discipleship Ministries   www.TeamWorksUMC.org

How to use the Spiritual Life Template

1. Ask one person to be the recorder, to take notes on the responses of each member. This is to be brought back at the next meeting to refresh everyone's memories.
2. Each person takes turns sharing which areas they want to focus on until the next time the group meets. On Question 1: Pick one area of focus. On Question 2: Also pick only one thing (do not pick one thing from each of the four areas)
3. Each person chooses for themselves what they will focus on.
4. Each person is asked to give specific details. For example, if someone says, "I am going to pray daily." A good follow-up would be to ask, "How much time?" The response may be, "15 minutes in the morning."
5. At the next meeting of the group, everyone shares what happened and they will have an opportunity to continue the same practice or to choose something different.
6. The group is to listen without judgment and to encourage people to try new disciplines.

Discipleship Ministries   www.TeamWorksUMC.org

Sample

1. In what spiritual discipline(s) do you want to grow?

Person 1: "I will read the Bible for 10 minutes in the morning each day."
Person 2: "I am going to do a media fast on Tuesdays."
Person 3: "I am going to say grace at dinner time with my family."

2. What is your continued plan for spiritual growth and development?

Person 1: "I am going to walk 30 minutes four times a week."
Person 2: "I am going to learn a new song on my guitar."
Person 3: "I am going to have an important conversation with a friend."

Discipleship Ministries   www.TeamWorksUMC.org

When the group gets together again

1. In what spiritual discipline(s) do you want to grow? How did it go? Do you want to continue or do something else?

Person 1: "I did fairly well. About 4 times a week. I want to see if I can get to six times a week this next time."
Person 2: "I loved my media fast. I am going to keep doing it."
Person 3: "If I could get my family to sit down together at the same time, I think we could say grace together. I'm going to try again."

2. What is your continued plan for spiritual growth and development?

Person 1: "I am going to bump it up to five times a week. I need to exercise."
Person 2: "I enjoyed getting back into my music. This time I will try walking four times a week for 30 minutes."
Person 3: "The conversation wasn't easy but it was good. Before our next time together we are going to meet at a coffee shop and see how it goes."

Discipleship Ministries   www.TeamWorksUMC.org

 # Discussion 4

- Ask each person to respond to the two questions on the *Spiritual Life Template*.

- When you finish go over the assignments before the next meeting and close with prayer.

Discipleship Ministries   www.TeamWorksUMC.org

Spiritual Life Template

1. In which spiritual discipline(s) do you want to grow?

__ Weekly worship
__ Daily Bible reading
__ Daily prayer
__ Frequency of communion:
　__ Weekly __ Monthly __ Other
__ Service to others
__ Fasting or abstinence
__ Tithing/Giving
__ Family prayer
Other:

Tip: How does your church teach & mentor people in these disciplines?

Wesley's Means of Grace

- **The public worship of God**
- **The ministry of the Word, either read or expounded**
- **The Lord's Supper**
- **Family and private prayer**
- **Searching the Scriptures**
- **Fasting or abstinence**
- **Christian conferencing**

2. What is your plan for your continued spiritual growth and development?

How do you connect with God?

__ Day apart
__ Worship
__ Meeting with a prayer partner or coach
__ Family prayer
__ Daily devotion
Other: _____

How are you connecting with others?

__ Time alone with spouse or friend
__ Focused time with your children
__ Regular connection with extended family
__ Prayer or accountability group
__ Time with friends outside of church
Other: _____

What arts feed your soul?

__ Playing a musical instrument or singing
__ Writing __ Drawing __ Cooking __ Dance
__ Gardening __ Acting Other:_____

How are you taking care of your body?

__ Walking/running __ Active in a sport
__ Healthy diet __ Yoga/Pilates
__ Other: _____

Tips

As a spiritual leader you are creating the normative expectations for spiritual growth in your congregation and for those close to you (friends & family). Your prayer life, physical health, artistic pursuits, and relationships have a direct influence on the spiritual life of your church. Build in the time and experiences that sustains you and connects you to God and others.

Assignments

- Read the MyWork devotions before your next meeting.
- Read the article on *The Spiritual Life of the Leaders*.
- As part of MyWork 4 fill out *Discovering My Spiritual Gifts* and be ready to share your gifts.
- Keep track on how you are doing with questions you answered on the *Spiritual Life Template* and come to the next meeting to share your results.

- As a group set your time for your next meeting.

Discipleship Ministries   www.TeamWorksUMC.org

MyWork

Date:

_____

SPIRITUAL LIFE

What Are My Spiritual Practices?

Early Methodists were taught that through the means of grace they would grow in faith and in practice. Because of the belief in sanctification (conversion as a lifelong process of being perfected in love), the means of grace were used as guidelines for Christian formation and growth.

Begin your time by taking the following Spiritual Leader Checklist, which is based on the means of grace. Answer the questions, and close with Bible reading and prayer.

Spiritual Leader Checklist

Points	Give yourself 10 points for each yes. 120 is the highest possible score.
	1. I say grace before each meal.
	2. I set aside a time to pray each day.
	3. At least once a week, I pray out loud with another person.
	4. I read at least one verse of Scripture every day.
	5. I attend worship at our church at least three times a month.
	6. At least twice a month, I meet with a small group of people to pray, reflect on Scripture, and build one another up.
	7. I take Communion at least once a month.
	8. At least once a month, I give of myself to others outside the church by volunteering at a homeless shelter, mowing a neighbor's lawn, visiting a nursing home, etc.
	9. I fast from food, media, or some other distracter once a week.
	10. I give financially to my local church on a regular basis with a goal of tithing.
	11. I have a regular plan of physical exercise to promote my health.
	12. At least once a month, I use my spiritual gifts for ministry at my local church.
	Total

Few people get a perfect score on this checklist. As you went through the list, what did you discover?

Are there areas for improvement?

What do you do on a regular basis that was not reflected on this list?

How have your practices changed over the years?

How do your spiritual practices inform your values?

Reflect on Psalm 1:1-3 and close in prayer.

*Happy are those
who do not follow the advice of the wicked,
or take the path that sinners tread,
or sit in the seat of scoffers;
but their delight is in the law of the Lord,
and on his law they meditate day and night.
They are like trees
planted by streams of water,
which yield their fruit in its season,
and their leaves do not wither.
In all that they do, they prosper.*

Before your next MyWork read the article on the "Spiritual Life of the Leaders" found on page 42.

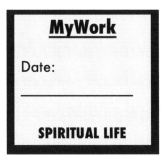

The Door

We use them every day. We open them. We close them.
We lock them. We knock on them. We stand outside them. We stand inside them.

They lock us in. They lock us out. They keep us safe. They keep us away. They say, "Welcome." They say, "Keep out."

They witness our comings and goings. They offer refuge when we are lost. They tell us when we are home.

Answer these questions about the door:

Where does the door go?

Who gets to walk through the door?

What is on the other side?

What keeps the door from opening?

Read the following passages:

Psalm 84:10-12
For a day in your courts is better
than a thousand elsewhere.
I would rather be a doorkeeper in the house of my God
than live in the tents of wickedness.
For the Lord God is a sun and shield;
he bestows favor and honor.
No good thing does the Lord withhold
from those who walk uprightly.
O Lord of hosts,
happy is everyone who trusts in you.

Revelation 3:15-20
I know your works; you are neither cold nor hot. I wish that you were either cold or hot. So, because you are lukewarm, and neither cold nor hot, I am about to spit you out of my mouth. For you say, "I am rich, I have prospered, and I need nothing." You do not realize that you are wretched, pitiable, poor, blind, and naked. Therefore I counsel you to buy from me gold refined by fire so that you may be rich; and white robes to clothe you and to keep the shame of your nakedness from being seen; and salve to anoint your eyes so that you may see. I reprove and discipline those whom I love. Be earnest, therefore, and repent. Listen! I am standing at the door, knocking; if you hear my voice and open the door, I will come in to you and eat with you, and you with me.

Reflect on what these passages say about the door and close in prayer.

MyWork

Date:

_____

SPIRITUAL LIFE

The Essentials

The call to follow God is one of the most profound concepts in biblical thinking. Two people come to mind: Abram, who was called to leave his home and to become the leader of a great people, and Mary, the mother of Jesus, who was called to give birth to the Son of God.

Read the following Scriptures and answer the questions. Then look at the passage from Acts 2 and answer the questions as well.

Abram's Call in Genesis 12:1-4
Now the LORD said to Abram, "Go from your country and your kindred and your father's house to the land that I will show you. I will make of you a great nation, and I will bless you, and make your name great, so that you will be a blessing. I will bless those who bless you, and the one who curses you I will curse; and in you all the families of the earth shall be blessed." So Abram went, as the LORD had told him; and Lot went with him. Abram was seventy-five years old when he departed from Haran.

Mary's Call in Luke 1:34-38
And Mary said to the angel, "How can this be, since I am a virgin?"
And the angel said to her, "The Holy Spirit will come upon you, and the power of the Most High will overshadow you; therefore the child to be born will be holy, he will be called the Son of God. And now, your relative Elizabeth in her old age has also conceived a son; and this is the sixth month for her who was said to be barren. For nothing will be impossible with God." Then Mary said, "Here am I, the servant of the Lord; let it be with me according to your word." Then the angel departed from her.

Here are a few things that jump out:

1. Neither Abram nor Mary had an official religious title such as priest or prophet. They were ordinary people. Many in the church think that a call is just for the clergy, but God calls all who choose to follow.

2. They each had a choice. Abram and Mary could have said no. Abram could have stayed in his hometown, and Mary could have said she did not want to give birth to the Son of God.

3. Once they said yes, God provided for them and gave them what they needed to complete the task. Neither was without its difficulties or struggles, but in the end, God's mission for them was fulfilled.

4. The call they received benefited others. Through Abram's obedience, the Hebrew people were established. Through Mary's acceptance, she brought into the world the Son of God. In both cases, all the people in the world were blessed.

Reflection Questions

1. What do the stories of Abram and Mary say to you about who is called?

2. As you first began your journey of faith, who helped you on the way?

3. How are you living out your call today?

Acts 2:37-42

Now when they heard this, they were cut to the heart and said to Peter and to the other apostles, 'Brothers, what should we do?' Peter said to them, 'Repent, and be baptized every one of you in the name of Jesus Christ so that your sins may be forgiven; and you will receive the gift of the Holy Spirit. For the promise is for you, for your children, and for all who are far away, everyone whom the Lord our God calls to him.' And he testified with many other arguments and exhorted them, saying, 'Save yourselves from this corrupt generation.' So those who welcomed his message were baptized, and that day about three thousand persons were added. They devoted themselves to the apostles' teaching and fellowship, to the breaking of bread and the prayers.

On the day of Pentecost, the crowd who listened to Peter talk about the resurrection of Jesus asked, "What shall we do?" Peter responded by sharing the basics. "Repent, and be baptized every one of you in the name of Jesus Christ so that your sins may be forgiven; and you will receive the gift of the Holy Spirit."

The passage tells us that once we believe and are baptized, we are given the Holy Spirit. It is the Holy Spirit who gives us the wisdom and the power to live out our call. We do not serve just on our own power. We serve because of God's grace. The rest of this passage tells us something else: our faith is not a solo affair. We are given the gift of community as well. As a result, we do not serve alone; we are called to serve together.

Reflection Questions

1. What do you think it means to receive the gift of the Holy Spirit?

2. How do we confirm one another's call in the midst of Christian community?

3. What does it mean for you to serve with others?

Reflect on Psalm 139:1-6 and close in prayer.

O Lord, you have searched me and known me.
You know when I sit down and when I rise up; you discern my thoughts from far away.
You search out my path and my lying down, and are acquainted with all my ways.
Even before a word is on my tongue, O Lord, you know it completely.
You hem me in, behind and before, and lay your hand upon me.
Such knowledge is too wonderful for me; it is so high that I cannot attain it.

MyWork

Date:

_____

SPIRITUAL LIFE

Discovering My Spiritual Gifts

Spiritual gifts are attributes given to Christian believers for the building up of the whole Body of Christ. Ephesians 4:11-13 says, "The gifts he gave were that some would be apostles, some prophets, some evangelists, some pastors and teachers, to equip the saints for the work of ministry, for building up the body of Christ, until all of us come to the unity of the faith and of the knowledge of the Son of God, to maturity, to the measure of the full stature of Christ."

Three points are especially important:

1. The use of spiritual gifts provides life and vitality to individuals and to the congregation. By using your spiritual gifts, you are contributing to the spiritual health of the church.

2. When an individual neglects to use his or her spiritual gifts, the whole community suffers.

3. When an individual is doing ministry in an area he or she is not gifted for, this leads to dissatisfaction on his or her part and hurts the whole community.

Where do spiritual gifts come from?

In Acts 2:38, Peter responds to the people who ask what they must do to be a follower of Jesus. He responds by saying, "Repent, and be baptized every one of you in the name of Jesus Christ so that your sins may be forgiven; and you will receive the gift of the Holy Spirit." In this statement, we find a fantastic promise: When we give our lives to Jesus Christ, we receive more than forgiveness and eternal life. We also are filled with the Holy Spirit, whose role in our lives is to provide us with guidance and power for living this life. As a result, we are given spiritual gifts that allow us to find our place in God's community of faith. As we employ these gifts in daily living, we find fulfillment and purpose in our relationship with God and with others.

How do I discover my spiritual gifts?

First, you need to know what they are. The Spiritual Gifts Assessment on page 40 covers twenty of the spiritual gifts found in Romans 12:6-8, I Corinthians 12:7-11, and Ephesians 4:11-13. Spiritual gifts are not limited to the ones used in this assessment. Gifts such as hospitality, tongues, music, and others can be found in the Bible. The more you learn about your gifts, the better you are able to use them. More importantly, you will discover those gifts that do not fit you, which means you need others to work with you.

Second, you need to have your gifts confirmed by the community of faith to see how your gifts benefit the whole congregation.

Third, you have to try out your gifts. That's where our energy for ministry comes from. Growing communities of faith give people multiple opportunities to find where their gifts best fit to build up the whole church.

What are primary gifts and enhancing gifts?

Your spiritual gifts are not set in stone. We all have a mixture of gifts that work together and give each of us a unique way to contribute to ministry. The primary gift is your strongest gift and oftentimes the one people will most easily confirm. The enhancing gifts are attributes we can explore. In many instances, they become the most important ways we contribute to the work of the whole ministry.

Spiritual Gift Assessment Tool

Use the Spiritual Gift Assessment Tool on the next page to get you started. This is meant as an introduction to the topic of spiritual gifts. Those of you who have taken spiritual gift inventories before can use this as a quick refresher. For those new to the idea of spiritual gifts, this will get you started in exploring this whole area of your spiritual life.

Instructions:

Step 1: Prayerfully read through these descriptions of spiritual gifts as taken from Romans 12:6-8, 1 Corinthians 12:7-11, and Ephesians 4:11-13.

Step 2: List two gifts from each category that best describe you, and write them in the boxes that are provided.

Step 3: Prayerfully look at the eight gifts you selected in Step 2, and put the one gift that best describes you in the #1 box below. This is your primary gift. In the other three boxes, list the next top three gifts that best describe you. These are your enhancing gifts.

Step 4: Share your results with people who are close to you and see what they think. There are numerous books and websites that you can use to learn more about this important topic.

Be sure to bring your results to the next seminar.

SPIRITUAL GIFT ASSESSMENT TOOL
Follow Steps 1, 2, and 3 as you discern your spiritual gifts.

ONE: PRAYERFULLY READ THROUGH THESE DESCRIPTIONS OF SPIRITUAL GIFTS AS FROM ROMANS 12:6-8, 1 CORINTHIANS 12:7-11, AND EPHESIANS 4:11-13.

SUPPORTING GIFTS: GIFTS THAT ARE USED TO SUPPORT OTHERS IN MINISTRY		TWO: LIST TWO GIFTS FROM EACH CATEGORY THAT BEST DESCRIBE YOU.
GIVING	I love to generously give of my financial resources to support ministry that transforms lives.	
ADMINISTRATION	I enjoy overseeing the overall aspects of a project or a task	**SUPPORTIVE**
HELPS	I receive satisfaction in assisting the work of others	1.
SERVICE	I find fulfillment in helping hurting people	2.
FAITH	I have an unshakable belief that God is in the midst of what is happening	
LEADERSHIP GIFTS: GIFTS THAT PROPEL THE VISION AND VALUES OF A MINISTRY		**LEADERSHIP**
PASTORING	I enjoy giving direction to the spiritual life of a group of people so they grow in faith	1.
TEACHING	I am able to share the truths of the gospel so they are easily understood	2.
PREACHING	I share the gospel in such a way that people grow into the vision and values of the congregation	**COMPASSIONATE**
LEADING	I know how to motivate and bring people together to achieve common goals	1.
APOSTLE	I find fulfillment in leading and overseeing a group of faith communities	2.
COMPASSIONATE GIFTS: GIFTS THAT MINISTER TO THE PHYSICAL, EMOTIONAL, AND MENTAL NEEDS OF PEOPLE		**SPIRITUAL LIFE**
HEALING	I have the ability to bring together all that is needed to heal people	1.
MERCY	I have great compassion for people who are hurting	2.
MIRACLES	I recognize God's intervention in a situation	
DISCERNMENT	I am able to help people make sense of difficult situations and give spiritual direction	**THREE:** WRITE YOUR TOP GIFT, YOUR PRIMARY GIFT, IN BOX #1. LIST YOUR NEXT TOP THREE, YOUR SUPPORING GIFTS, IN THE BOXES BELOW.
EVANGELISM	I enjoy sharing the gospel in a way that naturally leads people to have faith in Jesus	
SPIRITUAL LIFE GIFTS: GIFTS THAT ENHANCE THE SPIRITUAL LIFE OF THE MINISTRY		**#1 PRIMARY GIFT**
WISDOM	I have the ability to say the right thing at the right time to enable people to move forward in their lives	1.
KNOWLEDGE	I have great insight that comes from a close relationship to God	**SUPPORTING GIFTS**
PROPHECY	I am able to share God's call for a specific people that connects with their context	1.
TONGUES	I easily speak in languages that are different from my native language and effectively connect with people of different cultures	2.
INTERPRETATION	I am able to help people express their deep feelings about their faith	3.

Spiritual Gifts Results

1. What did you discover about yourself?

2. What implication does this have for your call?

3. How might this change or enhance what you are already doing?

4. How does this inform where you should put your energy and time?

Please bring your Spiritual Gift Assessment results with you to share at the next TeamWorks Seminar.

Reflect on Psalm 103:1-5 and close in prayer.

Bless the Lord, O my soul,
and all that is within me,
bless his holy name.
Bless the Lord, O my soul,
and do not forget all his benefits—
who forgives all your iniquity,
who heals all your diseases,
who redeems your life from the Pit,
who crowns you with steadfast love and mercy,
who satisfies you with good as long as you live
so that your youth is renewed like the eagle's.

SPIRITUAL LIFE OF THE LEADER
Seminar 2: Our Giftedness Together

Read Corinthians 12:4-7.

Now there are varieties of gifts, but the same Spirit; and there are varieties of services, but the same Lord; and there are varieties of activities, but it is the same God who activates all of them in everyone. To each is given the manifestation of the Spirit for the common good.

Reflection Question

The gifts are given for the common good. Share a couple examples of people in your ministry who use their gifts in ways that usually go unnoticed.

• How do these people impact the whole congregation?

• What motivates them?

• What would happen if they no longer served?

Discipleship Ministries   www.TeamWorksUMC.org

Spiritual Life Questions

1. In which spiritual discipline(s) do you want to grow?

___ Weekly worship
___ Daily Bible reading
___ Daily prayer
___ Frequency of communion:
    ___ Weekly ___ Monthly ___ Other
___ Service to others
___ Fasting or abstinence
___ Tithing/Giving
___ Family prayer
Other:

Tip: How does your church teach & mentor people in these disciplines?

Wesley's Means of Grace

- The public worship of God
- The ministry of the Word, either read or expounded
- The Lord's Supper
- Family and private prayer
- Searching the Scriptures
- Fasting or abstinence
- Christian conferencing

Discipleship Ministries   www.TeamWorksUMC.org

Spiritual Life Questions

2. What is your plan for your continued spiritual growth and development?

How do you connect with God?

___ Day apart
___ Worship
___ Meeting with a prayer partner or coach
___ Family prayer
___ Daily devotion
Other: _____

How are you connecting with others?

___ Time alone with spouse or friend
___ Focused time with your children
___ Regular connection with extended family
___ Prayer or accountability group
___ Time with friends outside of church
Other: _____

What arts feed your soul?

___ Playing a musical instrument or singing
___ Writing ___ Drawing ___ Cooking ___Dance
___ Gardening ___Acting ___Other:_____

How are you taking care of your body?

___ Walking/running ___ Active in a sport
___ Healthy diet ___ Yoga/Pilates
Other: _____

Discipleship Ministries   www.TeamWorksUMC.org

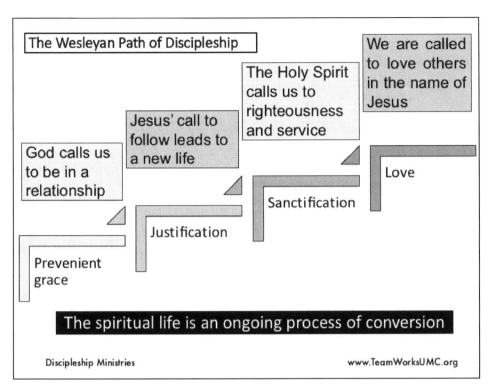

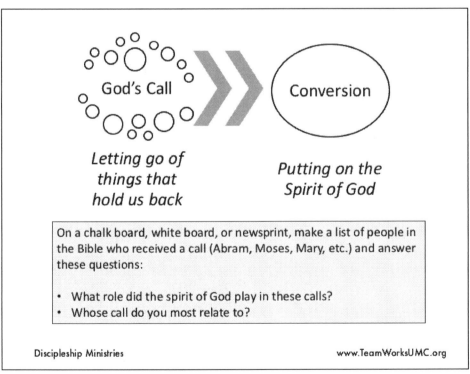

Spiritual Gifts Discernment

1. Ask group members to circle their primary gift on the *Spiritual Gifts Chart* pictured on the next slide.

2. Put check marks next to Supporting Gifts.

Personal Reflection:

How are my gifts distributed in the chart?

Do my gifts tend to fall more into one area than another?

What does this tell me about which is my strongest area?

How do my primary and supporting gifts work together?

When I think of working with others on a ministry team, what gifts of others will complement my gift mix?

Discipleship Ministries   www.TeamWorksUMC.org

SPIRITUAL GIFTS CHART

- Giving
- Administration
- Helps
- Service
- Faith

SUPPORTING   LEADERSHIP

- Pastoring
- Teaching
- Preaching
- Leading
- Apostle

SPIRITUAL LIFE   COMPASSION-ATE

- Wisdom
- Knowledge
- Prophecy
- Tongues
- Interpretation

- Healing
- Mercy
- Miracles
- Discernment
- Evangelism

Discipleship Ministries   www.TeamWorksUMC.org

Compile Your Spiritual Gifts Assessments

Have each team member take out his or her Spiritual Gifts Assessment.

On a white board, a chalkboard, or newsprint, draw the graph below.
(You need two colors of markers or chalk.) As you go around the table,
have each person share their Primary Gift. Write the answer under one
of the categories below. Next, using a different color, have each person
share his or her Supporting Gifts as they are placed on the chart.

Discipleship Ministries   www.TeamWorksUMC.org

Discussion 1

Look at the Spiritual Gifts Groupings and answer the following:

• How are the members of your group or team located in the groupings?

• Are you all in the same section?

• Are you dispersed throughout all four sections?
  Is one or more section empty?

• What does this tell you about the strengths of your group?
  Of your church?

• What does this tell you about where your congregation might need to
  grow?

• What excites you about what you have learned about yourself?
  About your team? Your small group? Your church?

Discipleship Ministries   www.TeamWorksUMC.org

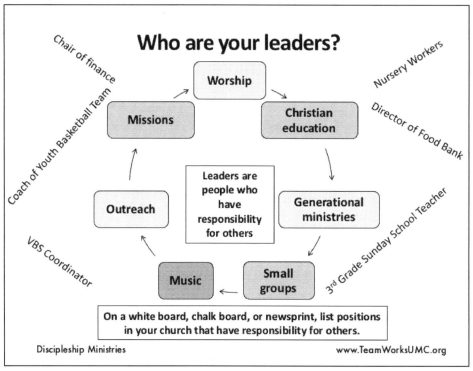

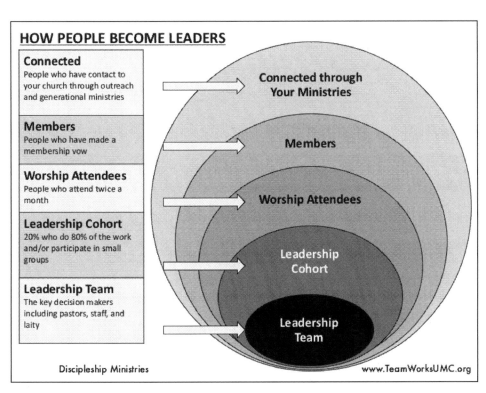

HOW PEOPLE BECOME LEADERS

Connected
People who have contact to your church through outreach and generational ministries

Members
People who have made a membership vow

Worship Attendees
People who attend twice a month

Leadership Cohort
20% who do 80% of the work and/or participate in small groups

Leadership Team
The key decision makers including pastors, staff, and laity

Connected through Your Ministries

Members

Worship Attendees

Leadership Cohort

Leadership Team

Discipleship Ministries   www.TeamWorksUMC.org

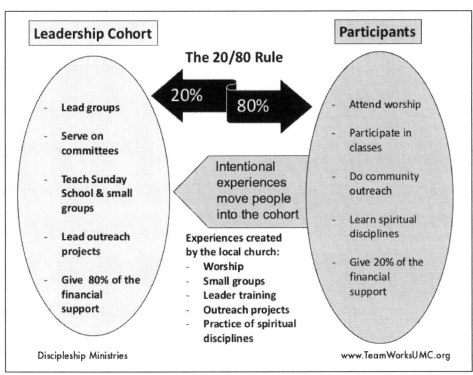

Leadership Cohort

Participants

The 20/80 Rule

20% 80%

- **Lead groups**
- **Serve on committees**
- **Teach Sunday School & small groups**
- **Lead outreach projects**
- **Give 80% of the financial support**

Intentional experiences move people into the cohort

Experiences created by the local church:
- **Worship**
- **Small groups**
- **Leader training**
- **Outreach projects**
- **Practice of spiritual disciplines**

- Attend worship
- Participate in classes
- Do community outreach
- Learn spiritual disciplines
- Give 20% of the financial support

Discipleship Ministries   www.TeamWorksUMC.org

 **Discussion 2**

- Who is in your Leadership Team?
- Who makes up your Leadership Cohort?
- Why are small groups part of the Leadership Cohort?
- In what ways are you equipping your Leadership Cohort?
- How are you inviting people to move through the system?

Discipleship Ministries www.TeamWorksUMC.org

What Strong Teams Have in Common

1. **Conflict does not destroy strong teams because strong teams focus on results.**

2. **Strong teams prioritize what's best for the organization and then move forward.**

3. **Members of strong teams are as committed to their personal lives as they are to their work.**

4. **Strong teams embrace diversity.**

5. **Strong teams are magnets for talent.**

Source: Tom Rath & Barry Conchie, *Strengths Based Leadership*, p. 71 - 75

Discipleship Ministries www.TeamWorksUMC.org

Followers' 4 Basic Needs

1. Trust	Do you do what you say and say what you do?
	Honesty, Integrity, Respect
2. Compassion	Do you care about those who work with you as real people?
	Caring, Friendship, Happiness, Love
3. Stability	Can people count on you in times of need?
	Security, Strength, Support, Peace
4. Hope	Do you initiate rather then react?
	Direction, Faith, Guidance

Source: Tom Rath & Barry Conchie, *Strengths Based Leadership*, p. 82 - 91

Discipleship Ministries   www.TeamWorksUMC.org

 **Discussion 3**

• How do you see your leaders living out the ideas presented in "What strong teams have in Common"?

• Where can there be improvement?

• What is the most helpful information from "Followers' Four Basic Needs"?

• What implications does this have for your ministry?

Discipleship Ministries   www.TeamWorksUMC.org

The Fruit of the Spirit is Available to All

While each of us has a particular spiritual gift mix, each of us also has the opportunity to live out of the fruits of the spirit. Galatians 5:22-26 (NRSV) says, "By contrast, the fruit of the Spirit is love, joy, peace, patience, kindness, generosity, faithfulness, gentleness, and self-control. There is no law against such things. And those who belong to Christ Jesus have crucified the flesh with its passions and desires. If we live by the Spirit, let us also be guided by the Spirit. Let us not become conceited, competing against one another, envying one another."

Discipleship Ministries   www.TeamWorksUMC.org

 Discussion 4

THE ROLE OF THE FRUIT OF THE SPIRIT

1. Why is it important to realize that everyone is to live out of the fruit of the spirit?

2. How can competition or envy undercut the ability of people to fully use their spiritual gifts?

3. How does avoiding conceit remind us that all gifts come from God?

4. What are some of the best ways to support one another as we discover and try out our spiritual gifts?

Discipleship Ministries   www.TeamWorksUMC.org

Next Steps

- Identify a group of leaders who will use the *Spiritual Life Template* as part of their regular meetings. This could be a staff team, a leadership team, a committee or a small group.

- Decide if you want more than one group to start using it.

- Talk about ways to use the *Spiritual Gifts Assessment* with leaders in your church.

- Create a process for developing your leadership cohort.

- Consider using another TeamWorks guidebook.

Discipleship Ministries   www.TeamWorksUMC.org

TeamWorks Guidebook Series: Tools for Creating Vital Faith Communities

Spiritual Life of the Leaders
- Encourage spiritual growth with the *Spiritual Life Template*
- Maximize your teams giftedness by discovering spiritual gifts

Connecting with Your Community
- Learn how new arrivals in your community seek *Homeland*
- Use the *NICHE Process* to learn about your community

Creating a Discipleship System
- Find out where your church fits on the *Lifecycle of the Church*
- Use the *Settings for Ministry* to form a discipleship system

Futurecasting
- Learn how to use the powerful *VAP→IT Strategic Planning Tool*
- Use the *TeamWorks Church Assessment* to plan for the future

www.TeamWorksUMC.org

Spiritual Life of the Leaders

Craig Kennet Miller

A couple of years ago I took a group of pastors to CalArts, one of the top arts colleges in the country. Located in the hills above the Rose Bowl in Pasadena, California, it attracts students from around the world who want to focus on the creative processes of art, dance, design, film, and writing. The topic of our conversation with Mitchell Kane, Director of Fine Arts, was on creativity. I'll always remember his opening remarks to the group, "You must be crazy!" Of course we were surprised by his remark, but once he elaborated he got to some very important points. He said something like this, "So you are responsible for creating fifty-two one-act performances a year that incorporate music, Scripture, and the arts along with a speech that inspires people to be more like God. I don't know how you do it."

When we think of it in those terms, leading worship and leading a church truly are daunting tasks. Besides worship, a pastor has the challenge of leading people with various opinions, backgrounds, values, grudges, and hopes. All who come to the church come because they want to be there. Add to the mix the increasing competition of the multimedia world we live in, and you wonder why anyone would want to do such a thing. Yet, every week in over 300,000 Christian churches in the United States, some brave soul with a heart for God gets up in front of a congregation and shares his or her passion for Jesus Christ.

Throughout the church, there is an ongoing debate about the nature of the church and of the conflict between clergy and laity in local congregations. Much of this comes as a result of the vast changes that are shaking up the culture as a whole and, in turn, the lives of those who make up the body of Christ.

As a result, leading a congregation is becoming more and more difficult. Pastors of local congregations find themselves operating in the midst of rapid cultural shifts and they are challenged to change or else. Many who are faced with declining and aging congregations wonder whether they will ever be able to make the changes necessary to lead their church in a different direction.

On the other hand, some lay members of congregations are tired of new pastors coming to their church and trying the latest fad while making them feel like what they have been doing has been worthless. Or they are longing for something new, when the existing pastor is content to do it the same old way.

Additionally, clergy and laity alike are increasingly stressed out by life in the fast lane. On top of the pressures at work and school, families find themselves on the front line of the cultural wars that surround them. Divorce and separations are just as likely to happen in clergy and church families as in the culture at large. Stress over the roles of men and women, finances, and the use of time stretch our capacity to love and care for one another.

These pressures and issues do not suddenly disappear when people show up at church. In many cases conflicts in the church are fueled by the disappointments and struggles of living in the 21st Century.

Rather than focusing on the heart of what is going on, we tend to focus on the symptoms. We argue over styles of worship, over the kinds of music we should play, over finding the right curriculum that mirrors our values, and how to reach those "new people" who have moved into the community. But what is overlooked in these debates is a far deeper issue: how do we treat one another and what is in our hearts.

My contention is that what is at the heart of many of the conflicts and issues that divide us is an inability to trust and to love one another. Before a congregation can grow spiritually and numerically, before it can effectively reach new people, it has to perform open-heart surgery; it has to look at its reason for being and at how its leadership team is living out the Christian faith.

The Leadership Cohort

In every congregation, there is a leadership cohort. A cohort is a group of people who share similar characteristics, like age, economic status, and culture. The leadership cohort in a church is made up of the dedicated people who share the same Christian beliefs and values, have a clear purpose, and who find meaning in serving through the church.

In the business world, there is a principle known as the 80-20 rule, also known as the law of the vital few. The principle states that 20% of your work results in 80% of your outcome. When we apply this to the church, we see that approximately 20% of the people give 80% of the financial support, and 20% of the people do 80% of the work.

The leadership cohort is your 20%. This cohort is made up of the leaders of the congregation who invest themselves in the life of the congregation. They may lead small groups and Bible studies, serve on committees and teams, or are active in the worship life of the congregation. They may sing in the choir, usher, or serve as liturgists. They may lead mission projects to help the poor, teach Sunday school, or serve as youth leaders. These are the people who are seriously committed to the life of the church and find meaning and purpose in what they do.

The way this leadership cohort works together, prays together, and encourages one another affects the whole life of the church. Its vision of what the church is supposed to be like, its hopes for the future, and its core values are seen throughout the life of the church.

HOW PEOPLE BECOME LEADERS

47

Ideally, the pastor and church staff are seen as part of this cohort. Like the laity, they have a stake in the future of the congregation. They, too, bring values, beliefs, and spiritual gifts to the table.

When a new person becomes the pastor of an existing church, the first job of the leadership is to create a healthy leadership cohort. This is the responsibility of both the laity and the pastor. Why? Because the relationships between people in the leadership cohort are the key to the future ministry of the congregation. As it says in Matthew 7:16-20:

You will know them by their fruits. Are grapes gathered from thorns, or figs from thistles? In the same way, every good tree bears good fruit, but the bad tree bears bad fruit. A good tree cannot bear bad fruit, nor can a bad tree bear good fruit. Every tree that does not bear good fruit is cut down and thrown into the fire. Thus you will know them by their fruits.

This passage of Scripture brings home a point that is often missed in the goal of creating vital congregations: If the tree is rotten, it cannot produce new fruit. If it's healthy, it produces new fruit in abundance. What is at the heart of the congregation affects the whole ministry and witness of the congregation. To say it another way, if the leadership cohort of the congregation hates one another, the congregation is going nowhere. If the leadership cohort loves one another, the future can be built on a solid foundation.

The Fruit of the Spirit and the Nature of Relationships

The fruit of the Spirit is not just for individuals; it gives us a picture of what our relationships are meant to be. The fruit of the Spirit tells us how we should interact and treat one another. As one grows in spiritual maturity, one's life is to be infused with the fruit of the Spirit. The fruit of the Spirit, like a cluster of grapes, is made up of a number of characteristics that, when seen together, give us an image of the attributes of a follower of Jesus Christ: *"The fruit of the Spirit is love, joy, peace, patience, kindness, generosity, faithfulness, gentleness, and self-control"* (Galatians 5:22–23).

When John Wesley talked about "going on to perfection," this is what he was pointing to: A Christian lifestyle marked by the fruit of the Spirit. These attributes are not given to us in an instant. We are to grow into them as we mature in faith. These attributes are at the heart of healthy relationships, the kind of relationships that encourage the believer and congregation alike to grow in faith and action.

How do the leadership cohort and the congregation move in this direction? Once again, Galatians 5:25–6:2,10, offers insightful advice:

If we live by the Spirit, let us also be guided by the Spirit. Let us not become conceited, competing against one another, envying one another. My friends, if anyone is detected in a transgression, you who have received the Spirit should restore such a one in a spirit of gentleness. Take care that you yourselves are not tempted. Bear one another's burdens, and in this way you will fulfill the law of Christ...So then, whenever we have an opportunity, let us work for the good of all, especially for those of the family of faith.

It is fascinating to see how focused these words of wisdom are on the way Christians are to treat one another. Paul's emphasis on the inward life of the congregation should cause us to ask why the way we treat one another is so important. For Paul, it is important because our witness to those outside of the faith depends on the nature of our relationships to one another as people of faith.

One of the keys to being effective in ministry is that what you say and do is real. *Real* is seen in the way people treat one another: Do they love one another? Do they treat one another with respect? Do they pray for one another? Do they pray every day? Do they seek God's will in all they do? Do they help those who are in need? How do they treat one another when conflict arises? Does adversity divide them or cause them to seek God's will as they work together for the common good?

The goal of tending to relationships is not to avoid conflict. In fact, conflict is a natural part of human relationships. When we work together, we will have differences of opinions; we will see things from different perspectives, sometimes even opposite points of view. That is how it is supposed to be! Sometimes the dissenter in the group has the answer or the right solution that everyone else has been unable to see.

The question for the leadership cohort of a local church is not how to avoid conflict; instead it's how to treat one another when conflict happens. Adversity brings out the true nature of our relationships with God and with others. Through adversity and change, the congregation is challenged to grow in understanding, faith, and trust.

In the bestselling book *Switch*, Chip Heath and Dan Heath make the case that rather than using crises to motivate people, positive emotions bring about lasting and fruitful change. While negative emotions narrow people's opinions and options, positive emotions "broaden and build" our thoughts and emotions.

They say, "Joy, for example, makes us want to play. Play doesn't have a script; it broadens the kinds of things we consider doing. We become willing to fool around, to explore or invent new activities....The positive emotion of interest broadens what we want to investigate....To solve bigger, more ambiguous problems, we need to encourage open minds, creativity, and hope."[1]

When seen in this light, conflict is an opportunity to discover new paths and new ways of working together. A leadership cohort who has invested time in spiritual disciplines and in having fun together, is best positioned to see conflict as a way to view situations from a new perspective.

[1] Heath, Chip, Heath, Dan; *Switch: How to change things when change is hard*, Broadway Books, New York, 2010, p. 122-123.

Basic Building Blocks of the Christian Life

A leader starting a new church comes to it with the expectation that new participants in the community of faith must be taught the "basics" of living as Christians. Prayer, Bible study, small groups, and missional outreach projects form the values and beliefs of those new to the Christian faith. Leaders do not expect new believers to act like believers until these new Christians have been shown the basic practices of the Christian life. Leaders do not assume that all people already know the basics of the Christian lifestyle.

As a result, leaders of new churches prepare materials to teach new believers the basics of the Christian lifestyle. They teach people how to pray. They help people discover their spiritual gifts. They show people how to have a daily devotion. They put people in places of outreach where they can begin to see God's work in the lives of other people. They show people how to worship from the heart. Even more important: The leaders live these basics themselves, or the whole thing just doesn't ring true.

Unfortunately, many existing churches operate on the assumption that their members already know the basics of the Christian life. But if prayer and Bible study have not been part of a congregation's life in years, on what basis do congregations make that assumption?

It may seem simplistic and obvious that the way you develop a healthy leadership cohort —and, as a result, a healthy congregation—is by learning the basics of the Christian life and living it out. But many leaders skip this step to get

on with the "real" business of the church, like creating new worship services or new ministries to the poor. But they skip this step at their own peril. Without a solid leadership cohort, the whole church can fall apart at the first sign of disappointment or conflict.

Investing in Your Leaders

Vital congregations invest in their leaders. They encourage them to grow in their spiritual disciplines; they give them opportunities to learn together; they give them the tools they need to do their job; and they have fun.

They make the equipping of believers for ministry a high priority. Second Timothy 3:16-17 says, *"All scripture is inspired by God and is useful for teaching, for reproof, for correction, and for training in righteousness, so that everyone who belongs to God may be proficient, equipped for every good work."*

Ephesians 4:11-13 carries the same theme: *"The gifts he gave were that some would be apostles, some prophets, some evangelists, some pastors and teachers, to equip the saints for the work of ministry, for building up the body of Christ, until all of us come to the unity of the faith and of the knowledge of the Son of God, to maturity, to the measure of the full stature of Christ."*

The critical emphasis in both these passages is this: Leadership equips believers to be in ministry. The job of the leader and the leadership team is not to do the ministry on behalf of others. Instead, the goal is to infuse people with the passion to be in ministry in the world and to give them the tools so they can be successful.

You may ask, "How do we create a healthy leadership cohort?" A couple of things can move you toward developing this leadership team:

1. Share the information in this chapter. Help people see that conflict over these issues is a natural part of the development of the leadership team.

2. Second, help the leadership team determine what spiritual practices they are going to commit to as leaders of the congregation. How often will they pray? What does faithful worship attendance look like? Do they read the Bible? How often? In order words, have the leaders look at Wesley's means of grace and ask what this means for their life together. (You may use the Spiritual Life Template for this)

3. Third, hold one another accountable. At the beginning of each leadership meeting, ask one another about your spiritual life.

4. Fourth, spend the beginning of each committee meeting, task group, or team session with a time of prayer, Bible study, and reflection. Fifteen to twenty minutes of this at the beginning is not wasted time. It is a time to focus people on why they are there in the first place.

5. Develop clear job descriptions with timelines, responsibilities, expectations, to whom they report, and the amount of time expected to do this job so people who are in leadership positions have a clear understanding of their commitment.

The pastor also must agree to the same commitments the leadership team makes and must be willing to be held accountable to the same criteria as the rest of the leadership team. When the pastor is vulnerable and willing to confess his or her struggles and successes it brings a refreshing change to the dynamic of leadership. Leaders are real people in the service of God.

Healthy Leadership Builds Healthy Churches

In both new and existing churches, leadership makes or breaks the future of the local congregation. Leadership that focuses first on developing a healthy leadership cohort best positions the congregation for change and moving into the future. This process may take from one to four years, depending on the situation the church finds itself in. This process of developing leadership is not for the impatient. It takes time, prayer, confidence, and dependence on the Holy Spirit to move beyond issues related to buildings and programs to focus on forming healthy Christian relationships that nourish the soul and create a strong foundation for spiritual and numerical growth.

Critical to the process are leaders, both lay and clergy, who are willing to say, "I need to grow in love and compassion." Leaders who do not have all the answers but have a desire to work with others to discover the answer are ones who create an atmosphere where healthy relationships develop. Healthy leaders create healthy leadership cohorts and, in turn, healthy congregations.

The Rev. Dr. Craig Kennet Miller is the Director of Congregational Development at Discipleship Ministries of the United Methodist Church. He is the author of iKids: Parenting in the Digital Age and Boomer Spirituality: Seven Values for the Second Half of Life. He is the designer of the TeamWorks resources and team member for the School of Congregational Development.

Spiritual Life Template

1. In which spiritual discipline(s) do you want to grow?

__ Weekly worship
__ Daily Bible reading
__ Daily prayer
__ Frequency of communion:
    __ Weekly __ Monthly __ Other
__ Service to others
__ Fasting or abstinence
__ Tithing/Giving
__ Family prayer
    Other:

Tip: How does your church teach &
mentor people in these disciplines?

Wesley's Means of Grace

- **The public worship of God**
- **The ministry of the Word, either read or expounded**
- **The Lord's Supper**
- **Family and private prayer**
- **Searching the Scriptures**
- **Fasting or abstinence**
- **Christian conferencing**

2. What is your plan for your continued spiritual growth and development?

How do you connect with God?

__ Day apart
__ Worship
__ Meeting with a prayer partner or coach
__ Family prayer
__ Daily devotion
    Other: _____

How are you connecting with others?

__ Time alone with spouse or friend
__ Focused time with your children
__ Regular connection with extended family
__ Prayer or accountability group
__ Time with friends outside of church
    Other: _____

What arts feed your soul?

__ Playing a musical instrument or singing
__ Writing __ Drawing __ Cooking __ Dance
__ Gardening __ Acting   Other:_____

How are you taking care of your body?

__ Walking/running __ Active in a sport
__ Healthy diet   __ Yoga/Pilates
__ Other: _____

Tips

As a spiritual leader you are creating the normative expectations for spiritual growth in your congregation and for those close to you (friends & family). Your prayer life, physical health, artistic pursuits, and relationships have a direct influence on the spiritual life of your church. Build in the time and experiences that sustains you and connects you to God and others.

SPIRITUAL GIFT ASSESSMENT TOOL   Follow Steps 1, 2, and 3 as you discern your spiritual gifts.

ONE: PRAYERFULLY READ THROUGH THESE DESCRIPTIONS OF SPIRITUAL GIFTS AS FROM ROMANS 12:6-8, 1 CORINTHIANS 12:7-11, AND EPHESIANS 4:11-13.		
SUPPORTING GIFTS: GIFTS THAT ARE USED TO SUPPORT OTHERS IN MINISTRY		**TWO:** LIST TWO GIFTS FROM EACH CATEGORY THAT BEST DESCRIBE YOU.
GIVING	I love to generously give of my financial resources to support ministry that transforms lives.	
ADMINISTRATION	I enjoy overseeing the overall aspects of a project or a task	**SUPPORTIVE**
HELPS	I receive satisfaction in assisting the work of others	1.
SERVICE	I find fulfillment in helping hurting people	2.
FAITH	I have an unshakable belief that God is in the midst of what is happening	
LEADERSHIP GIFTS: GIFTS THAT PROPEL THE VISION AND VALUES OF A MINISTRY		**LEADERSHIP**
PASTORING	I enjoy giving direction to the spiritual life of a group of people so they grow in faith	1.
TEACHING	I am able to share the truths of the gospel so they are easily understood	2.
PREACHING	I share the gospel in such a way that people grow into the vision and values of the congregation	**COMPASSIONATE**
LEADING	I know how to motivate and bring people together to achieve common goals	1.
APOSTLE	I find fulfillment in leading and overseeing a group of faith communities	2.
COMPASSIONATE GIFTS: GIFTS THAT MINISTER TO THE PHYSICAL, EMOTIONAL, AND MENTAL NEEDS OF PEOPLE		**SPIRITUAL LIFE**
HEALING	I have the ability to bring together all that is needed to heal people	1.
MERCY	I have great compassion for people who are hurting	2.
MIRACLES	I recognize God's intervention in a situation	
DISCERNMENT	I am able to help people make sense of difficult situations and give spiritual direction	**THREE:** WRITE YOUR TOP GIFT, YOUR PRIMARY GIFT, IN BOX #1. LIST YOUR NEXT TOP THREE, YOUR SUPPORING GIFTS, IN THE BOXES BELOW.
EVANGELISM	I enjoy sharing the gospel in a way that naturally leads people to have faith in Jesus	
SPIRITUAL LIFE GIFTS: GIFTS THAT ENHANCE THE SPIRITUAL LIFE OF THE MINISTRY		**#1 PRIMARY GIFT**
WISDOM	I have the ability to say the right thing at the right time to enable people to move forward in their lives	1.
KNOWLEDGE	I have great insight that comes from a close relationship to God	**SUPPORTING GIFTS**
PROPHECY	I am able to share God's call for a specific people that connects with their context	1.
TONGUES	I easily speak in languages that are different from my native language and effectively connect with people of different cultures	2.
INTERPRETATION	I am able to help people express their deep feelings about their faith	3.

Additional Resources

www.umcdiscipleship.org

The Discipleship Ministries site has resources for starting new churches, leading your church, ministering to people, and living the United Methodist way. It also is the gateway to the Upper Room Bookstore and numerous resources for worship, stewardship, evangelism, and leader development.

www.umcdiscipleship.org/webinars

This is your connection to an ongoing collection of webinars that covers all the essential areas of congregational life. Webinars on stewardship, worship, laity, church leadership, children's ministry, older adult ministry, congregational development and numerous other topics are offered by Discipleship Ministries staff to create vital congregations.

www.scdumc.org

This is your link to The School of Congregational Development, the annual congregational development event in August. Sponsored by Discipleship Ministries, Path 1, and The General Board of Global Ministries, the 4-day event gives congregational leaders and teams practical steps for developing missional disciple-growing faith communities.

www.TeamWorksUMC.org

This is your portal to the TeamWorks site at Discipleship Ministries. Here you will find TeamWorks seminars, downloadable presentations, and information on how to use these

TeamWorks Guidebook Series: Tools for Creating Vital Faith Communities

Spiritual Life of the Leaders

- Encourage spiritual growth with the *Spiritual Life Template*
- Maximize your teams giftedness by discovering spiritual gifts

Connecting with Your Community

- Learn how new arrivals in your community seek *Homeland*
- Use the *NICHE Process* to learn about your community

Creating a Discipleship System

- Find out where your church fits on the *Lifecycle of the Church*
- Use the *Settings for Ministry* to form a discipleship system

Futurecasting

- Learn how to use the powerful *VAP→IT Strategic Planning Tool*
- Use the *TeamWorks Church Assessment* to plan for the future

DISCIPLESHIP MINISTRIES
The United Methodist Church

73878141R00033

Made in the USA
Columbia, SC
23 July 2017